A CYNIC'S GUIDE TO LOVE

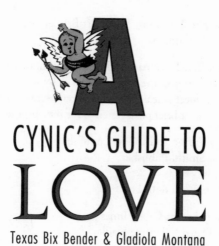

A
CYNIC'S GUIDE TO
LOVE

Texas Bix Bender & Gladiola Montana

GIBBS·SMITH
P
PUBLISHER

SALT LAKE CITY

First Edition

99 98 97 96 95 6 5 4 3 2 1

Text copyright © 1995 by Texas Bix Bender and
    Gladiola Montana

This is a Peregrine Smith Book, published by
    Gibbs Smith, Publisher
    P.O. Box 667
    Layton, Utah 84041

Designed by Leesha Gibby Jones
Edited by Dawn Valentine Hadlock
Cover illustration by Cary Henrie

LIBRARY OF CONGRESS CATALOG-IN-PUBLICATION DATA

Bender, Texas Bix, 1949-
A cynic's guide to love / Texas Bix Bender and Gladiola
    Montana.
p.   cm.
ISBN 0-87905-696-7 (pbk. : alk. paper)
1. Love—Quotations, maxims, etc. 2. Love—Humor.
    I. Montana, Gladiola. II. Title.
PN6084.L6B45   1995
302.3—dc20   95-19158
                                CIP

Printed and bound in the United States of America

Whoso loves
believes the impossible.

—Elizabeth Barrett Browning,
1806–1861

The first lover's
sigh says good-bye
to good sense.

*W*hat poets
and idiots call the heart
is located
a whole lot lower
than the left ventricle.

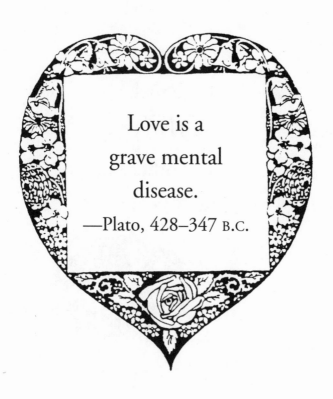

Love is a
grave mental
disease.

—Plato, 428–347 B.C.

Love makes

IDIOTS

out of otherwise

smart people.

Nine-tenths of what
we call the

*glory of
Love*

is really the glory
of imagination.

Mourning the loss of someone
we love is happiness
compared with having
to live with someone we hate.

—La Bruyére, 1645–1696

*Y*ou fall in love,
but you
don't fall out of it—
you get pushed!

Love is like
the measles—
all the worse
when it comes
late in life.

—Douglas Jerrold, 1803–1857

Anytime there's a choice
in love, it's a bad one.

15

Weddings are the
easy part and
should never be
celebrated—
it's anniversaries
that are notable.

Love is a

CRIME

that requires an accomplice.

—Baudelaire, 1821–1867

Love to a black widow spider
is short, sweet, and results
in a good dinner for the survivor.
Love to a human is long, bitter,
and there are no survivors.

Love isn't blind; it's stupid.

Every time you fall in love
you are the consummate
optimist—you think your
heart is full, when your
HEAD IS EMPTY.

Love is like money—
it's easier to
make it
than to keep it.

*S*cratch
a lover and find a foe.

—Dorothy Parker, 1893–1967

No one has ever loved
anyone the way
everyone wants to be loved.

Falling in love

twice

is a triumph of love over
experience.

—Dr. Johnson, 1709–1784

LOVE IS A
HEART ATTACK.

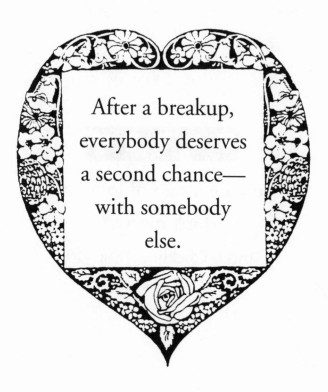

After a breakup,
everybody deserves
a second chance—
with somebody
else.

If you are afraid of loneliness,
don't marry.

—Anton Chekhov, 1860–1904

Love is the only game in which
two can play and both can lose.

'Tis better to have loved
and lost—much better.

Falling out a window
is easy compared to
falling out of love.

They call it
the "Wedding March"
because two people
are heading off to war.

—Ben Hecht

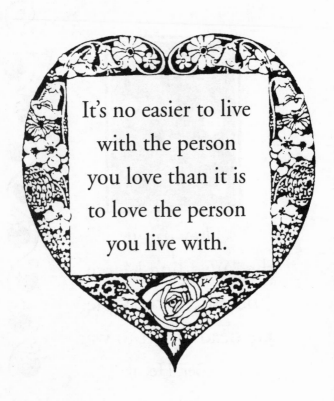

It's no easier to live
with the person
you love than it is
to love the person
you live with.

Love is a

castle built

of sand

and sooner

or later

the damned tide

comes in.

There is nothing like desire
for preventing the things
we say from having
any resemblance to the things
in our minds.

—Marcel Proust, 1871–1922

The magic of love is our
ignorance that it could ever end.

If you think you're falling in love,
think again.

Most people fall in love
in light so dim they wouldn't
buy a suit in it.

—Maurice Chevalier,

1888–1972

$\mathcal{L}$ove is like
a second-rate hotel:
it has a nice facade,
but the room service stinks.

Love is the delusion that
ONE IDIOT
differs from another.

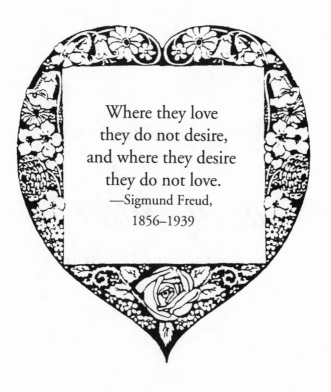

Where they love
they do not desire,
and where they desire
they do not love.
—Sigmund Freud,
1856–1939

Love seldom dies from
starvation—it's

indigestion

that generally does it in.

Most people in love confuse
excitement and stupification.

It's better to think of love as a gamble
rather than an insurance policy.

*I*t takes patience
to appreciate domestic bliss.

—George Santayana, 1863–1952

Love is a big, bright, blue
balloon in a world
of straight pins.

41

Love is a

LOT OF NOISE

from nothing more than

A LITTLE PAIN

IN THE ASS.

Love is a hole in the heart.

—Ben Hecht

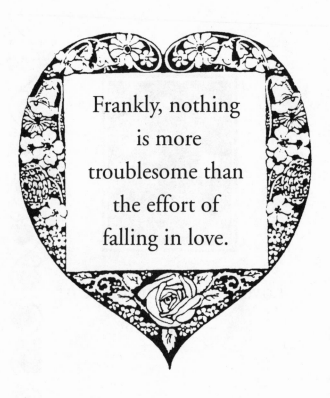

Frankly, nothing
is more
troublesome than
the effort of
falling in love.

Love requires
the greatest amount of
insincerity
possible between
two human beings.

Love is like an abscessed tooth:
It aches while you have it; still,
you miss it when it's gone.

Say it with flowers, say it with eats,

Say it with kisses, say it with sweets,

Say it with jewelry, say it with drink,

But always be careful not

to say it with ink.

*W*hile
black widow spiders
eat their lovers,
humans prefer to just
eat their own hearts out.

Only two kinds
of people understand love—
simpletons and liars.

All of us learn
to fall in love
by the sixth grade,
but most of us go
on to better things.

The difference between

LOVE AND MARRIAGE

is the difference between
lightning and a lightning bug.

—Bjorn Bob

(with apologies to Mark Twain)

Love is a peculiar situation in which
two idiots are adrift at sea, yet both of them
believe they are firmly in control.

Learning to love someone is
an acquired taste, like brussels sprouts.

The love that lasts longest
is the love that is

never
returned.

—Somerset Maugham,

1874–1965

There is no other
human activity that depends
so much on chance as love.

$\mathcal{I}$f you're sure
you are in love,
you're hopelessly confused.

True love is like

GHOSTS,

which everybody talks
about but few have seen.

—La Rochefoucauld, 1613–1680

Let us be happy while we may
And seize love with laughter;
I'll be true as long as you,
But not for a moment after.

Today's heart's
delight is
usually tomorrow's
delight that failed.

Puppy love

can lead to

a dog's life.

*L*ove
isn't everything;
there are also diamonds.

Lies lie in kisses.

Every woman should marry twice—
the first time for money
and the second time for love.
—Mrs. Oliver Belmont, mother of
the Duchess of Marlborough

Love is

LIKE A HOLE;

it's nothing in particular,
but you can break your neck
if you fall into it.

Usually before
love at first sight
comes cocktails
and twilight.

In matters of love,
there is nothing more persuasive
than courageous stupidity.

—Honorée de Balzac,

1799–1850

When a man loves a woman,
he can make her do anything

SHE WANTS TO.

Love is never a problem—it's the people you fall in love with who are the problem.

Love is affected by money only up to a certain point—a decimal point.

Politics doesn't make strange
bedfellows—marriage does.

—Groucho Marx

Lovers are always saying

they'll die

for you,

but they never do.

Who whines and begs
for love in humble mode
IS LIKE AN ASS
IN HARNESS,
braying for its master's load.

—Spanish proverb

First love
brings an end
to adolescent ignorance
and opens the door
to mature stupidity.

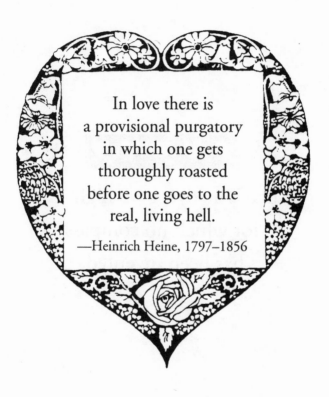

In love there is
a provisional purgatory
in which one gets
thoroughly roasted
before one goes to the
real, living hell.

—Heinrich Heine, 1797–1856

Love is a voyage on high seas
for which no compass
has been invented.

There is one person whom fate
has selected for each of us;
if we never meet them,
we are saved.

Never feel too guilty
over unkind thoughts about
someone you love; it's for sure
they've thought much
worse things about you.

I don't think there are any men who are faithful.

—Jacqueline Kennedy Onassis

Love is a story in which
the exciting part of the plot
dies in the first chapter.

Falling in love is like
giving someone
a bucket of paint
and inviting them
to paint you
into a corner.

*Give a man
a free hand*

and he'll run it all over you.

—Mae West

Everybody makes mistakes,
but that doesn't mean you
have to marry them.

You can live for love
and you can live in peace,
but you can't do both.

If you never say I love you,
you'll never have to
endlessly repeat it.

Men are like elephants to me:
I like to look at them,
but I wouldn't want
to take one home.

—Gloria Alred

*W*hen lovers tell you
that they agree with you
in principle,
what they mean is
that there will be iced tea
in hell before
you'll ever get your way.

Before you fall in love,

CHECK THE SPACE

behind your lover's eyes.

—Old Rumanian proverb

Opposites attract,
then do everything
they can to
pull apart.

Love means never
having your way again.

Your best bet for love
is to win the lottery.

There are four steps to

knowing a woman:

First, there is the affair;
next comes the marriage;
then the children;
and finally the fourth stage,
without which you
can never really know her,
the divorce.

—Norman Mailer

$\mathcal{S}$ure, fools fall in love,
but so do geniuses.
It's not brains; it's glands.

In love the big lie
is a lot easier to believe
than the small one.

It's a universal truth

that a person with
a fat bank account is in need
of a person to help spend it—
in the name of love, of course.

—Lily Latrobe, actress of sorts

Hearts are like eggshells,
born to be broken.

A single broken
heart is sad;
a million broken
hearts is
a hit country song.

*Love may
be a bargain,*
but as in any bargain,
somebody always gets
the short end of the stick.

Love is a universal migraine,
A bright stain on the vision,
blotting out reason.

—Robert Graves, 1895–1985

In love, the hors d'oeuvres are often better than the main course.

Love is the
whoopee cushion
of the heart.

You're incomplete
until you're in love,
and then you're finished.

If love is good,
from whence cometh
such woe?

—Chaucer, 1342–1400

Love is a dreamy
little island in an
ocean of reality,
and when the tide
comes in,
the island disappears.

Love doesn't
MAKE THE WORLD GO 'ROUND;
it makes it dizzy.

Love is simple if you're an idiot.

To keep your heart from breaking,
you have to bust your ass.
—Charlie Bill (songwriter, sports broadcaster)

You go

into love blind

and come out with

20/20 vision.

The problem with love is
that once somebody gives
you their heart,
you have to take all
the baggage
that goes with it.

September 8, 1942

Dear United States Army,

My husband can't read or write, that's why he's asked me, I'm his wife, to write this letter for him. He would like to be excused from being drafted because we need him to support us his family. Don't tell him, but no we don't. He stays drunk and gets in fights most every day. I got four of his kids to raise and am carrying anothern, I could do without him, without any problem. You're welcome to him. Let him raise hell with them germans.

—An unsigned letter given to the Kentucky draft board

When it comes to love,
take the fifth…

NAH, MAKE IT
A QUART.

Love is kind of like going
three rounds with
George Foreman:
if it doesn't kill you,
you're very careful about
who you get back
in the ring with next time.

Love is a very nerve-wracking
thing to be involved in;
you have to be

sweet and

smiley

to the same person
every damn day of the year.

—George Beatty

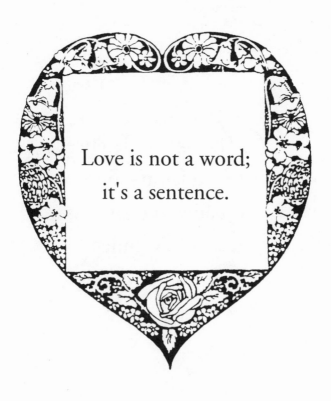

Love is not a word;
it's a sentence.

The only difference
between falling in love
and falling on your ass
lies in how much
you've been drinking.

When you're in love,
you'll listen to the biggest idiot,
fall for the biggest lies,
and ignore the greatest insults
you'll ever receive.

When you fall in love,
you give up the attention of many
for the inattention of one.

Falling in love is like buying

SOMETHING ON
IMPULSE:

It looks great when
you pick it out;
but when you bring it home,

IT JUST DOESN'T

go with anything.

—June Cleaver (all right, not really)

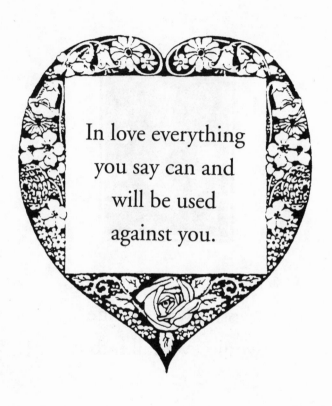

In love everything
you say can and
will be used
against you.

Love *must* be blinding,
otherwise no one
would ever fall into it.

Love is like a

*fiery bowl
of chili:*

Yes, it's good while it lasts,
but when it's gone you're
left with tears in your eyes,
feeling damned sorry you ever
took your first taste.

A man running after a hat
is not half so ridiculous
as a man running

AFTER A WOMAN.

—G. K. Chesterton, 1874–1936

(died hatless)

When a woman talks about
a man with a strong will,
she's referring to one
made out in her favor.

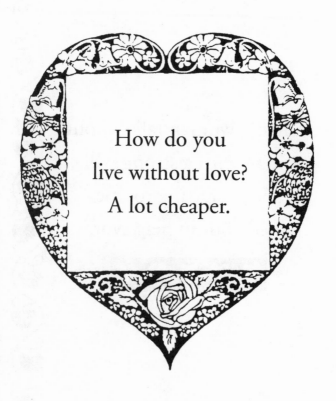

How do you
live without love?
A lot cheaper.

*M*any play
the game of love,
but few ever know
the score.

I LOVE
MICKEY MOUSE

more than any woman
I've ever known.

—Walt Disney, 1901–1966

Romance is fun
and games.
Love is war.

Love has the

amazing

reflective ability

to let you see someone appear
to be twice as good as they are,
or twice as bad.

Love is eating your own heart out,
and liking it.

Women are loved for
what they are, men for
what they promise to be.
—Goethe, 1749–1832

*M*en are
nicotine-soaked,
beer-besmirched,
whisky-greased,
red-eyed devils!

—Carry Nation, 1846–1911

Love can't be thought out or talked out; it has to wear out.

A new love is kind of like

A NEW PAIR
OF BOOTS:

you never know where
it's gonna pinch, you never know
where it's gonna rub a blister,
but you know it's gonna do both.

—Old Rome, Texas, saying

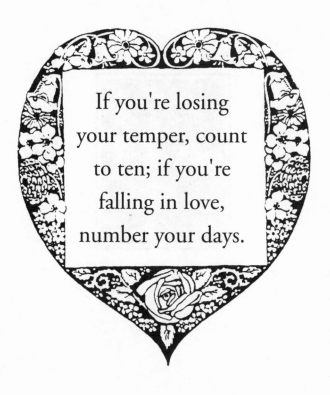

If you're losing
your temper, count
to ten; if you're
falling in love,
number your days.

Love is just another
of those four-letter words.

The big difference between

*a wedding
procession
and a funeral
procession*

is the music.

"I love you."
Yep, that's the biggest lie
anyone ever tells in their life.
—Henry Miller, 1891–1980

There is a giant difference
between the civilized and
uncivilized person in love,
but it narrows noticably when

THINGS GO AMISS.

Well, love is what it is.
As bad as it gets,
it's still better than its

opposite.

(Although not by as wide
a mark as one might think.)